REFUTATION OF THOSE WHO DO NOT FOLLOW THE FOUR SCHOOLS

Al-Radd ʿalā man Ittabaʿ Ghayr al-Madhāhib al-Arbaʿa

IBN RAJAB AL-ḤANBALĪ

REFUTATION OF THOSE WHO DO NOT FOLLOW THE FOUR SCHOOLS

Al-Radd ʿalā man Ittabaʿ Ghayr al-Madhāhib al-Arbaʿa

IBN RAJAB AL-ḤANBALĪ

Translation & Notes by

MUSA FURBER

IBN RAJAB'S REFUTATION OF THOSE WHO DO NOT FOLLOW THE FOUR SCHOOLS

ISBN 978-0-9858840-8-6 (paper)
ISBN 978-1-944904-01-2 (EPUB)

Published by: Islamosaic (publications@islamosaic.com)

بسم الله الرحمن الرحيم

All praise is to Allah alone, the Lord of the Worlds
And may He send His benedictions upon
our master Muhammad, his Kin
and his Companions
and grant them
peace

TRANSLITERATION KEY

ء	ʾ[1]	ر	r[6]	ف	f
ا	ā, a	ز	z	ق	q[13]
ب	b	س	s	ك	k
ت	t	ش	sh	ل	l
ث	th[2]	ص	ṣ[7]	م	m
ج	j	ض	ḍ[8]	ن	n
ح	ḥ[3]	ط	ṭ[9]	ه	h[14]
خ	kh[4]	ظ	ẓ[10]	و	ū, u, w
د	d	ع	ʿ[11]	ي	ī, i, y
ذ	dh[5]	غ	gh[12]		

1. A distinctive glottal stop made at the bottom of the throat. It is also used to indicate the running of two words into one, e.g., *bismi'Llāh*.
2. Pronounced like the *th* in *think*.
3. Hard *h* sound made at the Adam's apple in the middle of the throat.
4. Pronounced like *ch* in Scottish *loch*.
5. Pronounced like *th* in *this*.
6. A slightly trilled *r* made behind the upper front teeth.
7. An emphatic *s* pronounced behind the upper front teeth.
8. An emphatic *d*-like sound made by pressing the entire tongue against the upper palate.
9. An emphatic *t* sound produced behind the front teeth.
10. An emphatic *th* sound, like the *th* in *this*, made behind the front teeth.
11. A distinctive Semitic sound made in the middle throat and sounding to a Western ear more like a vowel than a consonant.
12. A guttural sound made at the top of the throat resembling the untrilled German and French *r*.
13. A hard *k* sound produced at the back of the palate.
14. This sound is like the English *h* but has more body. It is made at the very bottom of the throat and pronounced at the beginning, middle, and end of words.

CONTENTS

TRANSLITERATION KEY VI
TRANSLATOR'S PREFACE VIII
Ibn Rajab's Refutation 1
TRANSLATOR'S NOTES 21
BRIEF BIOGRAPHIES 31
ABOUT THE TRANSLATOR 34

TRANSLATOR'S PREFACE

In the Name of God, Most Merciful and Compassionate

I had a very productive translation spree from 2001 through 2004. It was during that period that I translated Imām al-Nawawī's *Etiquette With the Quran,* Abū Shujāʿ's *The Ultimate Conspectus,* Imām al-Juwaynī's *Al-Waraqāt* with al-Maḥallī's commentary, al-Buhūtī's *Zād al-Mustaqniʿ*, and others – including this translation of Ibn Rajab's *Refutation of Those Who Follow Other Than The Four Schools.*

About the author

Ibn Rajab is Abu al-Faraj ʿAbd ar-Raḥmān ibn Aḥmad, a well-known Ḥanbalī jurist and ḥadīth master. He was born in Baghdad in 1335 CE/736 AH and moved to Damascus at the age of five, and then to Jerusalem. He studied in Jerusalem, Mecca, and Egypt. He eventually returned to Damascus, where he taught students of his own. His sheikhs include al-Subkī, al-ʿIrāqī, and Ibn al-Qayyim al-Jawziyyah. He is most famous for his works pertaining to hadith, including his commentary on Imām al-Nawawī's *Forty Hadiths*. He started a commentary on *Ṣaḥīḥ al-Bukhārī* titled Fatḥ al-Bārī which he was not able to complete. Ibn Ḥajar gave his own commentary the same name out of honor for Ibn Rajab. His mastery of fiqh is evident in his book of legal maxims drawn from Ḥanbalī *fiqh*.

He passed away in 1393 CE/795 AH. May Allah shower him in His mercy.

TRANSLATOR'S PREFACE

About the essay

Ibn Rajab's *Refutation of Those Who Follow Other Than The Four Schools* is an essay advocating for the necessity of following Islamic scholarship in general, and legal scholarship in particular. The first half of the essay covers the history of the development of Islamic scholarship and how the Muslim Community came to recognize scholars as the source for authoritative knowledge. The second half offers advice to students of Sacred Knowledge – particularly those following the Ḥanbalī school.

Readers of the essay will notice that Ibn Rajab is engaging individuals who claim to be affiliated with a particular school of scholarship yet see themselves as equal or superior to its prior generations of scholars and free to cast aside their findings without themselves possessing the requisite skills and knowledge. Although written seven centuries ago, it might as well have written with today's 21th century ce reformers in mind.

The essay mentions many Companions, Successors, and Righteous Forebears (may Allah be pleased with them all and grant them His mercy). Short biographies for most of them are included in an appendix.

The translation has gone through numerous revisions and conversions. I was inexperienced when I translated it and it shows. I have tried to bring the main text closer to what I would do today. One area that remains particularly deficient is the lack of notes related to concepts such as modes and manners of recitation of the Quran [*ḥurūf* and *qira'āt*, respectively]. These (*in shā' Allāh*!) will be explained better in a forthcoming work on the sciences of the Quran.

May Allah reward Ibn Rajab. May Allah grant His mercy to all who read this essay, and may He make us among those who benefit from it. Where I have succeeded, it is only through His grace; where I have faltered it is from my own shortcomings.

Musa Furber
Abu Dhabi
June 30, 2015

This page left blank.

IBN RAJAB'S REFUTATION OF THOSE WHO DO NOT FOLLOW THE FOUR SCHOOLS

In the name of Allah, Merciful and Compassionate; through Him we seek aid.

Praise be to Allah, Lord of the worlds; a frequent, wholesome praise, blessing Him, as our Lord loves and is pleased by. May Allah bless Muḥammad, His slave and messenger, the unlettered Prophet, the seal of the Prophets, and Imam of the godfearing; the one delegated with the upright religion, and the lasting, assisted, protected legislation. [A protected legislation] which a group of his community will never cease triumphantly following the truth, unharmed by those who desert them, until the Final Hour comes.[1]

To commence:

Someone's rebuke has reached me: a rebuke for my censuring people today who affiliate with the school of Imām Aḥmad or another famous Imam, yet depart from their school in issues. He claimed that someone who does this is not to be reprimanded since he might be a *mujtahid*[2] following what appeared to him to be the truth or emulating another *mujtahid*, and that this, therefore, is not held against him.

So I say, and success is only with Allah; He is the One sought for help, reliance is upon Him, and there is no strength nor power except through Allah:

There is no doubt that Allah Most High has protected for this community its religion, a protection He has given none other. There is no prophet after this community to renew what has vanished from its religion, as it was for the religions of the prophets before us: whenever one vanished, another prophet would come after him to renew it.[3]

Allah Majestic guaranteed protection for this religion and affirmed that in every age there would be an offensive to expel from it the corruption of the extremists, tricks of the nullifiers, and interpretations of the ignorant.[4]

Allah Most High said, "Indeed We sent down the Remembrance and indeed We are protective of it" (Quran, 15:9), guaranteeing protection for His book. Thus, no one has been able to add to or remove from it a single phrase.

Protecting the Quran

During his time, the Prophet ﷺ recited the Quran to his community using different 'modes of recitation' [*ḥurūf*] to make it easy for them to memorize and learn it. His community included old men and women, young boys and girls, and men who had never read a single book. So, for their sake he ﷺ sought a facilitation for them memorizing it, reciting to them with seven modes of recitation [*ḥurūf*], just as it is related in the hadith of Ubay bin Kaʿb and others.[5] Then when the word of Islam spread in regions and the Muslims separated to distant lands, each group of them began reciting the Quran according to the mode of recitation that had reached them. They differed in the modes of recitation of the Quran and when they gathered during Hajj or other events, they differed greatly in [the pronunciation of some words in] the Quran.

During ʿUthmān's time, the Companions of the Prophet ﷺ agreed to gather the community on one mode of recitation, from fear that this community would disagree in its book as the previous communities had. They realized that public interest required it, and they burned the *maṣāḥif* of every other mode of recitation.[6] This was one of the good qualities for which 'Alī, Ḥudhayfa, and the prominent companions praise the Commander of the Faithful, ʿUthmān (may Allah be pleased with them).

During the time of the Prophet ﷺ ʿUmar (may Allah be pleased with him) fiercely criticized Hishām bin Ḥakīm bin Ḥizām over one verse, and a scribe who wrote revelation for the Prophet ﷺ whose faith was not firmly rooted in his heart recanted because of this until he died an apostate.[7]

What shall we assume of the community after him ﷺ, if there had remained between them differences in pronouncing the Quran?

So because of this the community's scholars of recitation abandoned everything other than the mode of recitation ʿUthmān gathered the Muslims under. Some of them made a dispensation in it:[8] an opinion is related from Aḥmad and Mālik, with their difference of opinion whether it is in prayer or other things, or prayer only.

In any case: The community does not disagree that if someone recited a canonical reading [like Ibn Masʿūd's] disagreeing with this agreed-upon muṣḥaf and claimed that the mode of recitation he recited is that of Zayd bin Thābit over which ʿUthmān gathered the community, or claimed that it was more worthy of recitation than Zayd's mode of recitation: then he is unjust, overstepping bounds, and deserving of punishment. Concerning this, no two Muslims disagree.

Indeed, the area of disagreement is if he reads with a letter like Ibn Masʿūd's despite acknowledging that it is the letter of Ibn Masʿūd which disagrees with the *muṣḥaf* of ʿUthmān (may Allah be pleased with them).

Preserving the Sunna

The sunnah of the Prophet ﷺ has been in the community and memorized in the hearts just like the Quran. Some of the scholars wrote it just as [they wrote] the *muṣḥaf*, while others prohibited writing it. And there is no doubt that people greatly differ in [their] memorization and accuracy.

Then, after the age of the Companions (may Allah be pleased with them) there came a people of innovation and misdirection. They introduced into the religion what was foreign to it and they intentionally lied about the Prophet ﷺ. To protect the sunnah, Allah Most High established a group of individuals to distinguish between the lies, whims, and mistakes. They corrected to the utmost limit, and memorized it to perfection.

Then the scholars compiled collections of the sunnah and compilations of hadiths, and its sciences spread. The scholars came to depend on the books of the two Imāms – Abū ʿAbdullāh al-Bukhārī and Abū al-Ḥussein [Muslim] bin al-Ḥajjāj al-Qushayrī (may Allah be pleased with them) – for rigorously authenticated [*ṣaḥīḥ*] hadith. After these, their reliance was on the rest of the books of the sunnah, especially Abū Dāwūd's *Sunan*, Abū ʿIsā's *Jāmiʿ*, al-Nasā'ī's book, and then Ibn Mājah's.

Other collections of authentic hadith were compiled after the sound books of the two Shaykhs [Imams al-Bukhārī and Muslim], however these collections did not reach the criteria of the two Shaykhs. Because of this, [some] scholars rebuked [al-Ḥākim] who supplemented their two books with the book he named *al-Mustadrak*. One of the hadith masters exaggerated, claiming that there is not a single hadith [in it] meeting their conditions [for judging a hadith to be authentic]. Another disagreed with him, saying that many sound hadiths are sifted from it. The fact is that many authentic hadiths are sifted from it that do not reach their conditions but do reach the conditions of Abū ʿIsā and the like; but as for their conditions: no.

It is very rare that both al-Bukhāri and Muslim left a hadith unless it contained a hidden defect. Because of the rarity of one who has knowledge like theirs regarding defects and criticism (a single person is not prepared except in far-apart ages!), and hence we depend on their two books: we trust and return to them, and then to the remaining books indicated above. After this, grading a hadith to be authentic or weak is not accepted except from someone whose knowledge, expertise, and being well-versed in this art are well known – and they are very rare. Everyone else relies on these indicated books and is satisfied tracing [hadith] back to them.

Preserving Legal Judgments

As for rulings and issues of the lawful and the prohibited: there is no doubt that the Companions, their Successors, and those after them (may Allah be pleased with them) had many disagreements concerning these issues. In the early times, anyone well known for knowledge and religion issued legal pronouncements according to what seemed to him to be the truth of these issues, and no one outside of this group [who did likewise] was free of censure from the scholars. It is like [when] Ibn ʿAbbās (may Allah be pleased with him) was censured over several issues about which he had a unique opinion.[9] His followers were censured even more than he was: when Ibn Jurayj came to Baṣra and the people of Baṣra saw him enter the main mosque, they raised their hands supplicating Allah against him because of his irregularity in the issues that he took from companions of Ibn Masʿūd (may Allah be pleased with him), until he recanted some of these opinions before departing from them. This was a time when the majority of the people were dominated by religion and scrupulousness.

This saved them from someone speaking without knowledge and those who claimed to possess knowledge while not being qualified. But then religion and scrupulousness declined. It became common for someone to speak without knowledge or claim it for himself while not being qualified. If the state of the earlier times – where everyone gave rulings according to what appeared to him to be the truth – had continued in the later times, it is inevitable that there would be no order in the religion, and the lawful would have become prohibited and the prohibited lawful. Everyone would have said what they wanted, and our religion would have become like the *ʿaqīdah* of the people of the two ooks before ours [the Jews and Christians].

So it is the wisdom of Allah Most High that [He] set the religion and protected it and appointed Imāms for the people: Imāms among the scholars of juridical opinion and hadith, whose knowledge, understanding, and arriving at the furthest goals in the ranks of knowledge of rulings and legal verdicts, are [all] agreed-upon. People came to rely upon them for legal verdicts and to refer to them for knowing judgments. Allah raised people who corrected their schools and formulated their principles until each Imām's methodology in jurisprudence, basic principles, and details were established; until the rulings were traced back to the basic principles concerning the issues of the lawful and the prohibited were established.

This is among Allah's gentle kindness toward His believing slaves, and among the mass of His customary laws in preserving this religion. If not for this, people would have seen the wonder of wonders: every imbecile, hot-headed, insolent, sham who was impressed with his opinion would claim that he is the greatest of all Imāms, that he is the one to guide the community, that people should turn only to him, and that no one else should be relied upon.

However, with praise for Allah and His gracious bestowal, this door of great danger and tremendous weight was barred. And this great corruption was constrained. This is among the gentle kindness, beautiful habits, and tender mercies of Allah Most High towards His slaves.

In spite of this, people still appear, claiming to have reached the level of *ijtihād*, speak about knowledge without restraint, or following one of those Imāms. This is tolerated from some of them because of the apparent veracity of their claims. For others, their statement is rejected and they are declared liars concerning their claim. As for everyone else who has not reached this level: they are only capable of following one of these Imāms and following what the rest of the community did.

An insolent imbecile might object, asking:

> *How can people be restricted to the opinions of designated scholars, and be barred from ijtihād or imitating one of the other scholars of the religion?*[10]

Our reply is that it is just like the Companions (may Allah be pleased with them) gathered the people in all the lands on one of the modes of recitation of the Quran and prevented them from reciting any other mode when they saw that the general interest would be incomplete without it, and that if the people were left reading various modes of recitation they would fall into the greatest of ruins.

Rulings and verdicts of the lawful and prohibited are just like this. If the people were not restricted to the opinions of the enumerated Imāms it would lead to corruption in the religion. Every insolent imbecile seeking personal leadership would consider himself included in the group of *mujtahids*. He could invent an opinion and attribute it to one of the early predecessors; perhaps it would be twisted, like what frequently took place from some of the Ẓāhiriya, and it might have been one of the predecessor's blunders that a group of them had agreed to abandon.

General welfare demands nothing other than what Allah destined and carried out in gathering the people of the schools of those well known Imāms (may Allah be pleased with them).

The difference between gathering the people on one of the seven modes of recitation and gathering them on the opinions of the four Imāms is that the meanings of those seven modes of recitation are said to be identical or close and these meanings are obtained by this [single] letter. This differs from the opinion of the four jurists, since it is possible for them to agree on something which lays outside the truth.

A group of scholars have denied this: that Allah surely will never gather this community upon misdirection. There are hadith supporting this.

But assuming that it could be true: it occurs rarely and only a mujtahid who has attained more than they have can notice it. This is absent or rare, and it is obligatory for this *mujtahid* – assuming his existence – to follow what appears to him to be the truth. As for everyone else, it is obligatory to follow [*taqlīd*], and following these Imāms is acceptable without a doubt. There is no sin upon them or anyone else who follows [all of] them or some of them.

But this leads to following some of the Imāms in a mistake.

An entire body of people does not say the truth, so inevitably one of those who disagrees must be reprehensible. Moreover, a mistake does not befall the community unexpectedly and would most often take place – if it does take place – in things that rarely occur. As for issues that Muslims are universally in need of: it is not permissible to believe that the Imāms who are followed in Islam throughout these lengthy ages have agreed upon a mistake, for this is a damning blemish on this community from which Allah has protected it.

We concede to preventing the general masses from following the way of ijtihād since this leads to the greatest of wrongs. However, we do not concede to preventing following an imitated, mujtahid Imām, outside of those famous Imāms.

We have pointed out the reasons for preventing this: it is that the other unpopular schools have not been corrected and perhaps something is attributed to them that they did not say, or understood [from them] that they did not intend. Their schools have no one to defend them and point out the mistakes that took place in them, contrary to these famous schools.

So what do you say about another Imām's school if it has been recorded, corrected, and memorized, just like their schools?

Firstly, this is not known to exist at the moment. If we assume that it did take place, and conceded the permissibility of following it and affiliating with it, this would not be permissible except for someone who visibly shows affiliation to it, gives verdicts according to it, and defends his school.

As for someone who outwardly shows affiliation to one of the famous Imāms while he is secretly affiliated with someone else, firmly believing in his school: this is absolutely impermissible. It is a form of hypocrisy and misrepresentation. This is especially the case if he took money restricted to the followers of that famous school, like from endowments; or deceived people, making them believe that the fatwa he gives from the school he secretly affiliates with is [really] from the school of the famous Imām.

This certainly is impermissible. It is a deception toward the community and a lie toward the scholars of the community.[11] Whoever attributes to the Imāms of Islam something they did not say, or something known to be contrary to what they say, is a liar worthy of punishment. It is the same if he had authored a book following a particular school mentioning in it a statement he believes to be from the Imām he secretly affiliates with while not attributing it to its [actual] proponent. And it is the same if the authored book is not confined to a specific school and the author outwardly affiliates with a particular Imām while secretly affiliating with another Imām and he mentions the opinion of the Imām with whom he secretly affiliates without clarifying that they disagree with the school he outwardly affiliates with.

All of this is impermissible fraud and deception, leading to tainting and confusing the scholars' schools.

If he also claims *ijtihād*, it is more crafty and bitter, and of greater corruption and pigheadedness. This is absolutely impermissible except for someone possessing the complete tools of *ijtihād*: knowing the Quran, sunnah, legal rulings of the Companions and the Successors (may Allah be pleased with them), knowing consensus and differences, and the rest of the well-known conditions for *ijtihād*. This requires much inspection of the sunnah, knowing its sound from its unsound, knowing the schools of the Companions and their Successors (may Allah be pleased with them), and the accounts related from them concerning this.

Because of this, Imām Aḥmad was strict in the matter of fatwa, and held back from it anyone who did not memorize one hundred thousand hadith, two hundred thousand, and more.[12] The indication of the proof of his claim is that concerning issues he was independent in his opinions, just like the other Imāms; his opinions were not taken from someone else. As for someone who relies solely on conveying someone else's words (whether it be the ruling or the ruling with evidence): the goal of his toil is to understand it. Perhaps he did not understand it well, corrupted it, or changed it. And how far this is from *ijtihād*! It is just as it was said:

> Stop writing, you have no business writing
>
> Even if you blotted your face with ink

So what do you say about Imām Aḥmad and other Imāms prohibiting others following them and recording their opinions. And what about Imām Aḥmad's statement, 'Do not record my words, nor the words of so-and-so and so-and-so. Instead, learn as we learned'? This is frequently found in their words.

There is no doubt that Imām Aḥmad (may Allah be pleased with him) used to prohibit probing the opinions of jurists and being preoccupied with memorizing and writing them. He would order being occupied with the Quran and sunna: memorizing, understanding, recording, and studying it; writing the accounts of the Companions and their Successors (may Allah be pleased with them): not the words of those after them, and knowing authentic and weak [reports]; that which is taken from, and the cast out, odd statement. There is no doubt that this is something that requires preoccupation with being learned before anything else.

Whoever knows this and reaches the furthest limits (as Imām Aḥmad pointed to): his knowledge will have become close to the knowledge of Imām Aḥmad. There is no restriction upon him and these words are not directed at him. Indeed the words concerning prevention are only for someone who has not reached this limit, did not rise to this end, and understood only an insignificant portion – as is the state of the people of this age. Indeed, this has been the state of most people for ages, despite many of them claiming to have reached the limits, and ending at the furthest extent, while most of them had not risen from the very beginnings.

Imam Aḥmad's Knowledge

To verify this yourself, look to the knowledge of Imam Aḥmad (may Allah be pleased with him) in the Quran and sunnah. As for his knowledge in the Quran, he (may Allah be pleased with him) paid much attention to the Quran, understanding it, and its sciences. He would say to his companions, "Indeed, people have abandoned understanding the Quran," in a manner of censuring them.

He gathered many books concerning the Quran, including *Kitāb al-Nāsikh wa al-Mansūkh* (*"Abrogated and the Abrogating Verses"*), *Al-Muqaddam wa al-Mu'akhkhar* (*"Transposed Verses"*). He gathered a large commentary of the Quran, containing exegesis from the Companions and their Successors (may Allah be pleased with them).

His commentary belongs to the type related from the Forebears: commentary from his Shaykhs, like ʿAbd al-Razzāq, Waqiʿ, Ādam bin Iyās, and others; commentary from his peers, like Isḥāq and others; and from those [born] after him whom he took from, like al-Nasā'ī, Ibn Mājah, Ibn Abū Ḥātim and others, from Ahl al-Ḥadīth. All of them gathered accounts related from the Forebears concerning commentary without adding their own opinions.

As for his knowledge (may Allah be pleased with him) of the sunnah, this matter is well known and widespread. There is agreement and consensus concerning it. Indeed: he bears the banner of sunnah and hadith, and is the most knowledgeable person of his age concerning the words of the Prophet ﷺ, his Companions, and their Successors (may Allah be pleased with them).

He was singled out in this from his peers by several matters, including [his] vast and abundant memorization. It is said that he memorized three hundred thousand hadiths.

What singled him out includes his knowledge of [distinguishing] sound narrations from the unsound. This is sometimes by knowing the trustworthy from the blemished, and he was the limit in the science of narrator commendation and discreditation [*jarḥ wa taʿdīl*]. Sometimes this is through knowledge of the paths of hadiths and their differences, and knowing the hidden defects of hadith [*ʿilal al-hadith*]. He was also the limit in this. Even if many hadith masters shared with him in knowing the defects of a raised chain (Prophetic) report [*marfūʿ*] attributed to the Prophet ﷺ, no one reached his knowledge in the defects of a severed chain [sub-Companion] report [*maqṭūʿ*], one attributed to anyone lower than him ﷺ. Whoever ponders his words concerning this sees wonders and is firmly convinced of how rare it is that anyone would reach his understanding in this science.

Part of what set him apart was his knowledge in the *fiqh* of hadith: understanding it, its [rulings concerning what is] lawful and the prohibited, and its meanings. He was also the most knowledgeable of his peers in this, just like the Imāms from his peers testified: Isḥāq [bin Raḥūyah], Abū ʿUbayd, and others.

Whoever ponders his opinions in *fiqh* and understands his approach and insights, knows the strength of his understanding and inferences. However, because of the subtlety of his words in this, it might be difficult for many of the Imāms who author books in his school to understand him, so they leave his subtle approach for other weak approaches adopted from people outside of their school. Because of this many disturbances take place in understanding his words and they misinterpret them. Students of his school need nothing other than careful scrutiny and understanding his discourse.

Things have been seen from his understanding and knowledge that are full of amazement. How would this not be so when there is no issue that the Companions and their Successors (may Allah be pleased with them) spoke about except that he knew it, his knowledge encompassed it, and he recognized the base of the issue and understood it? Likewise the words of the jurists from all regions and the Imāms of all lands: such as Mālik, al-Awzāʿī, al-Thawrī, and others. All of the knowledge and legal verdicts of those Imāms were read to him. He responded to them, sometimes agreeing, and sometimes disagreeing. Indeed, Muhanna bin Yaḥyā bin Manṣūr read to him all of the [legal] issues of al-Thawrī and he responded to them. A group read to him the issues of Mālik and his legal verdicts from *al-Muwaṭṭa'* and others and he responded to them. (Ḥanbal and others related this.) Isḥāq bin Manṣūr read to him all of the issues of al-Thawrī and he responded to them. In the beginning, he wrote the books of Abū Ḥanīfa's companions and understood them, their approach in jurisprudence, and their insights. He had debated al-Shāfiʿī and sat with him for a time and took from him.

Al-Shāfiʿī (may Allah be pleased with him) witnessed those great things in jurisprudence and knowledge while Aḥmad, in spite of this, was just a youth not yet at the height of his life.

It is known that it would be the easiest thing for someone who understood these sciences and excelled in them to know new issues and respond to them on the basis of these accurately mastered fundamentals and known approaches. Because of this Abū Thawr said, "Whenever Aḥmad was asked about an issue, it was as if the knowledge of the world was [written] on a board in front of his eyes" (or however it was said).[13]

We do not know an authentic sunnah from the Prophet ﷺ except that he encompassed it with his knowledge. He was the strictest of people in following the sunnah when it was authentic [*ṣaḥīḥ*] and unopposed by strong conflicting evidence. Indeed, he only abandoned taking what was not sound and was opposed by strong conflicting evidence.

Because of the close contact the Forebears (may Allah be pleased with them) had to the time of the prophecy and their frequent pursuit of the words of the Companions, Successors and those after them (may Allah be pleased with them), they knew the abhorrent hadiths that were not acted upon. They cast them aside and were content in following what the Forebears practiced. In this they knew things from the sunnah [via direct experience] that those after them reached [indirectly] only through books of hadith due to the length of time and their distance [from the sources].

Advice for Students

Once you understand and perceive this, then here is advice for you, O student of this Imām's school. I render this service to you purely for the pleasure of Allah, since "None of you believes until he loves for his brother that which he loves for himself":[14]

Do not think for even a moment of talking yourself into believing that you perceive something that this Imām was unaware of, or understood something that he did not reach – someone shown to have surpassed the most gifted of those after him. Put all of your efforts into understanding the words of this Imām concerning all the issues of knowledge, not [just] the issues of *islām* [the lawful and the prohibited].

In the science of belief (meaning the issues of belief in Allah, His angels, His books, His messengers [peace be upon them], and the final day), in the nomenclature of many scholars it is the science called 'knowledge of the sunnah.' Indeed, this Imām was the limit in this science. He was persecuted because of issues he had, and was patient for the sake of Allah during this inquisition. All Muslims were pleased with his stand and the position he took. They testified that he is the Imām of the sunnah, and if not for him the people would have disbelieved. Whoever holds this position in the science of the sunnah, how is it necessary – especially for those affiliated with his school – to obtain this knowledge through words from any other scholar?

So hold firmly to his words in everything under this subject, and turn away from the new matters that occurred in superfluous issues. Muslims have no need of what took place. Indeed, it preoccupies one from useful knowledge, places enmity and hatred between the Muslims, and results in much debate and argument in this life – [all of] which is prohibited according to this Imām and others from the past Forebears.

And likewise the science of iḥsān, the science of constant vigilance and humility. This Imām was the furthest extent in this, just as he was a divine sign [*āyah*] in *islām* and *imān*. However, in this matter he was a person of deeds, not waxing eloquently about spiritual states. Because of this he would utter only what was ascribed to the Forebears, not what the *Khalaf* [post-Succesors] contrived. In all of his sciences, he (may Allah be pleased with him) supported himself with the sunnah and did not subscribe to uttering opinions which the pious Forebears did not utter, especially in the sciences of *imān* and *iḥsān*.

As for the science of *islām*: he responded to new matters that had not been spoken about before because of the need for [a response], and despite prohibiting his companions from speaking concerning issues for which they have no reference. Usually, he only responded to what had been talked about previously; what is needed, and what [actually] occurs and must have a known ruling. As for the issues that the jurists contrived which take place rarely if at all: he frequently prohibited responding to them since they are of little benefit and preoccupy one from what is obligatory to know and more important.

He (may Allah be pleased with him) did not subscribe to much arguing and debate, nor making room for repeating what everyone says in any of the sciences, perceptions, and states. Indeed, he was satisfied with the sunnah and reports from the Companions (may Allah be pleased with them), and he encouraged understanding the meanings of the above without speaking long or much. He did not forsake making room for speaking (with thanks for Allah!) out of inability or ignorance, but out of scrupulousness, immense merit, and satisfaction with the sunnah. Indeed, following the sunnah and following the pious predecessors of the Companions and the Successors (may Allah be pleased with them) is a sufficiency, and guidance is obtained by following [them].

If you accept this advice and follow the sound path, make your aspiration memorizing the phrases of the Quran and sunna; then get acquainted with its meanings conforming to what the predecessors and Imāms of the community said. Then memorize the opinions and legal verdicts of the Companions and Successors (may Allah be pleased with them) and the opinions of the Imāms of the regions, and accurately mastering the words of Imām Aḥmad verbatim, knowing his meanings, and making decisive arguments according to his understanding and knowledge.[15]

If you reach the limit in these, do not assume that you have reached the end: indeed, you are just one student among many, and even if you had been present in the time of Imām Aḥmad, you would not even be counted among the mass of students. If you convince yourself after this that you are finished or reached what the Forebears reached, you are grossly mistaken.

Do not dare to neglect memorizing the sciences mentioned above and accurately mastering the texts and relied upon accounts and [instead] be preoccupied with much argument and debate, repeating what everyone says, and considering some statements more preponderant than others out of what your intellect prefers, while in reality you do not know who said those statements and whether he is among the Forebears whose statements have weight or from those who were compromised.

Do not dare to speak about the Book of Allah or a hadith from the Messenger of Allah ﷺ with anything other than what the Forebears said – as your Imām indicated – lest the beneficial knowledge pass you by and your days be wasted. Indeed, beneficial knowledge is what is set in the hearts and handed down from the Messenger ﷺ or the pious Forebears, not "What's your opinion?" and "My opinion is..." The Companions and the ones after them (may Allah be pleased with them) who lead to guidance when followed prohibited this. How is your claim of affiliating with an Imām sound, when you persist in contradicting him and flee from his sciences, his actions, and his path?

Know (may Allah give you success) that when you are occupied with this path, traveling the correct means of reaching Allah, employing *taqwa* (which is the same as vigilance), and looking to the states of the previous Imāms by continually looking at their state while assuming the best results – then your knowledge of Allah and His Divine order will increase. You will increase in belittling and having outrage at your lower self [*nafs*]. Moreover, you will have something from your self that keeps you preoccupied from being free to clash with the Muslims.

Do not pass judgment on all the divisions of the Believers, as if you were given knowledge that they were not, or attained a state that they did not. Allah has mercy towards someone who assumes the worst concerning his own knowledge, action and state, and assumes the best concerning the predecessors: someone who knows that deficiency is from himself and completeness is with the predecessors and does not pounce upon the Imāms of the religion, especially like Imām Aḥmad; and especially if he affiliates himself with him.

If you refuse this faithful advice and take the path of argumentation and disputation, committing what you were prohibited from doing in the way of libeling others [*tashadduq*], acting with pride and arrogance [*tafayhuq*], and mouthing brazen nonsense [*shiqshiqat al-kalām*][16] until your main preoccupation becomes the refutation of the Imāms of the Muslims and searching out their defects – all it will do is make your soul puff up with more conceit, increase your love for oppression in the earth,[17] distance you farther from the truth, and bring you all the more closer to falsehood. At that point you will ask, "Why should I not say what I say when I am more deserving than anyone else to speak and decide? Who is more knowledgeable than I? Who is wiser [*afqah*] than I?" [just] as mentioned in hadith literature. In this community, only someone who is fuel for the fire would say this!

May Allah protect us from this ignominy and give us success to accept this advice through His Graciousness and Generosity. Indeed, He is the Most Merciful and Most Gracious of all.

But if you continue persisting in believing that knowledge and understanding [*al-tafaqquh*] is quoting opinions, hair-splitting and arguing; believing that whoever accommodates this and hunts for the Imāms' defects by searching and seeking evidence is more knowledgeable than one who does not do this; and that one who has few words in this has not arrived – then we say this to you:

It is from here that some groups of the misguided believe that the Khalaf were more knowledgeable than the Forebears since the Khalaf differ [from the Forebears] in their frequent recording of everything everyone said. We free ourselves from these statements for the sake of Allah! If this were how it really is, the Shaykhs of the Mu'tazila and the Rāfiḍa would have been more knowledgeable than the Forebears and Imāms of the community!

Ponder the words of the Shaykhs of the Muʿtazilites like ʿAbd al-Jabbār bin Aḥmad al-Ḥamdānī and others, their abundant probing, debating, and the vastness of their numerous opinions, and [ponder] anyone from the people of theological disputation [*kalām*] from the other groups. And so are the authors from all other schools of theological disputation and in jurisprudence from all the schools: they are excessively verbose in every issue. Their own Imāms did not speak over these issues or in such detail and a verbose manner. So is it permissible because of this to believe their superiority over the Imāms of Islam, such as Saʿīd bin al-Musayyib, al-Ḥasn, ʿAtā', al-Nakhaʿī, al-Thaurī, al-Layth, al-Awzāʿī, Mālik, al-Shāfiʿī, Aḥmad, Isḥāq, Abū ʿUbayd, and the like? Rather, the Successors were more expansive in their statements than the Companions (may Allah be pleased with them) by far. And does any Muslim believe that the Successors are more knowledgeable than the scholars of the Companions (may Allah be pleased with them)?

Ponder stated of the Prophet ﷺ: "Belief is from Yemen, understanding is from Yemen, and wisdom is from Yemen."[18] He ﷺ said this in praise for the Yemenis and their merits. He testified that they have understanding and belief. He attributed it to them because of their having reached the furthest extent in understanding, belief, and wisdom [*fiqh, īmān, ḥikma*].

We know no other group of scholars of Muslims who speak less and are less argumentative than the Yemenis, whether from the Forebears or the Khalaf. This indicates that the knowledge and understanding praised in the language of the Lawgiver is knowledge of Allah which leads to loving Him, His love, glorifying Him, and venerating Him; they are included with the essential knowledge, and His orders and prohibitions. This is just as the scholars from the people of Yemen in the past were: Abū Mūsā al-Ashʿarī, Abū Muslim al-Khawlānī, Uways [al-Qaranī], and others, not like what others have added to it: jumbling people's words together and frequently searching out their hidden faults and mishaps.

It is true that most of the Imāms made mistakes in minor issues that do not diminish their station and knowledge. But so what? The mistake was engulfed by their goodness and abundant correctness, and the excellence of their objectives and their aiding the religion.

Appointing oneself as inquisitor of their lapses is neither praised nor thanked – especially in extraneous issues where a mistake does no harm – so there is no benefit to uncovering and exposing their mistakes. Similar to this is much searching and superfluous sciences that are not beneficial in the religion, distract one from Allah and being occupied with Him, harden the heart from His remembrance, and cause love of rank and leadership over people. None of this is praiseworthy. The Prophet ﷺ would seek protection from knowledge of no benefit.[19] He ﷺ said, "Ask for beneficial knowledge, and seek protection from knowledge which does not benefit."[20]

He ﷺ said, "Verily, there is a kind of knowledge that is [nothing but pure] ignorance."[21] He ﷺ disliked frequent, longwinded talk, and loved concision. There are many hadith concerning this, though it would be lengthy to mention them.

It is the same with occupying oneself to rebut the speech of the innovators using the same type of talk, using analogies and rational proofs. Imām Aḥmad and the Imāms of Ahl al-Ḥadīth (such as Yaḥyā al-Qaṭṭān, Ibn Mahdī, and others) disliked this. They only considered rebutting them with texts from the Quran, the sunnah, and the words of the previous Imāms if available. Otherwise they considered it safer to remain silent.

Ibn al-Mubārak and other Imāms would say, "To us, Ahl al-Sunnah are not the ones who rebut the people of whim, rather they are the ones who concerning them remain silent." He mentioned this out of dislike when they turned away from the knowledge that the Prophet ﷺ brought, and from the action it leads to. Indeed, it suffices. And whoever is not sufficed by it, may Allah never suffice him!

I know that people of debates and arguments most vehemently criticize and protest everything I mentioned here. But when the truth becomes clear it is necessary to follow it and abandon turning towards those who dispute it, cause dissension, argue, and incite.

From this it is known that the knowledge of Imām Aḥmad and the Imāms who traveled his path is the most true knowledge of all and the loftiest and highest sciences of the community, and that it contains a sufficiency for whomever Allah has guided to the truth.

"And whomever Allah has for him no light, what light has he?" (Quran, 24:40).

TRANSLATOR'S NOTES

1. The Prophet ﷺ declared that there will always be a group of Muslims who unwaveringly adhere to the truth. This was reported by at least sixteen Companions, including al-Mughīra, Thaubān, and Jābir (may Allah be pleased with them). For a complete list of reporters, see , #145. For sample reports, see Muḥammad ibn Ismā'īl al-Bukhārī, *Ṣaḥīḥ al-Bukhārī,* n.a., hadith number according to the Fatḥ al-Bārī edition, n.a., #7311; Muslim ibn al-Ḥajjaj, *Ṣaḥīḥ Muslim,* volume 5, Dār al-Fikr, Cairo, reprint of Maṭbaᶜa ᶜĪsā al-Bābī al-Ḥalabī, 1956 CE edition, 1983 CE, #157, 1920-21, 23; Aḥmad bin Ḥanbal, *al-Kitāb al-Musnad,* 5:278, 279; and others.
2. *Ijtihād* is when a qualified expert exercises their personal reasoning. A *mujtahid* is someone who is qualified to perform *ijtihād*. Please see *Matn al-Waraqāt* and *Sharḥ Matn al-Waraqāt* for more information. (Both are published by ISLAMOSAIC).
3. Allah Most High said, Muḥammad is not one of your men, rather he is the Messenger of Allah and the last of the prophets (Quran, 33:40). The Prophet ﷺ said, "Verily, there will be no prophet after me" *Ṣaḥīḥ al-Bukhārī,* #4416; *Ṣaḥīḥ Muslim,* 2404; Aḥmad bin Ḥanbal, *al-Musnad,* 1:182, 183; 3:338; 6:369, 438.
4. The Prophet ﷺ said, "The upright carry this knowledge from every successor. They deny the extremists' deviations, tricks of the nullifiers, and invalid interpretations of the ignorant" in a hadith narrated by Abū Hurayra, Abū Masᶜūd, ᶜAlī, Usāma bin Zayd, and Muᶜādh bin Jabal (may Allah be pleased with them).

[The numerals in the parenthesis are to be understood as follows: those set off by a colon (e.g.: 5:234) refer to volume and page number of the source; the others are the hadith numbers, as they are arranged in the respective hadith compendiums.]

5. These seven modes of recitation [*aḥruf*], according to one of the most well-known opinions, corresponded to the most popular Arabic dialects in use at the time of the Quran's revelation. Many of the differences between these modes were simply differences in pronunciations for the same word, without any substantial difference in the meaning. These seven modes of recitation are preserved through the well-known recitations [*qira'āt*], though there is not a perfect correspondence between the aḥruf and the canonical recitations that we see preserved today. This is not to suggest that the Companions recited the Quran however they liked, according to their colloquial dialect, as the content and recitation of the Quran are both part of its Revelation and both were transmitted from the Prophet ﷺ. So it is reasonable that a Companion who heard a verse directly from the Prophet ﷺ would be alarmed upon hearing another Companion reciting the same verse with a different mode (may Allah be pleased with them all). For examples, see *Ṣaḥīḥ al-Bukhārī,* #4991; *Ṣaḥīḥ Muslim,* #281, 819; Aḥmad bin Ḥanbal, *al-Musnad,* 1:264, 299, 313; 5:127, 129.
6. See *Ṣaḥīḥ al-Bukhārī,* 4987.
7. Ibn Rajab may intend ʿAbdullāh bin Saʿd bin Abī Sarḥ (may Allah be pleased with him), the first Qurayshi to write for the Prophet ﷺ. He did subsequently leave Islam, but he later returned on the day Mecca was conquered.
8. Ibn Masʿūd is reported to have made a dispensation. See al-Tirmidhī, Abū ʿĪsā, *Sunan al-Tirmidhī,* volume 5, Dār Iḥyā' al-Turāth al-ʿArabī, Beirut, reprint of Cairo edition edition, 3103.
9. These issues include temporary marriage. See al-Dhahabī, Muḥammad ibn Aḥmad, *Tadhkirat al-Ḥuffāẓ,* volume 4 in 2, Dār al-Ma'rifa, Beirut, n.d., 1:170-71; al-Dhahabī, Muḥammad ibn Aḥmad, *Mīzān al-Iʿtidāl fī Naqd al-Rijāl,* volume 4, Dār al-Maʿrifa, reprint, Beirut, 1382 ah, 2:659; , 6:331.
10. From here on, objections will be displayed inset and in italics.
11. See , p541.
12. cf. , p514.
13. I was not able to find this or a similar quote from Abū Thawr, not even when the author gives a summary biography for Imām Aḥmad in *Sharḥ al-ʿIlal.* Ibn Rajab himself added "or however it was said," hinting that he had questions about the wording, not the truth of the statement itself. Abu Thawr referred to Imām Aḥmad as "our Imām."

14. See *Ṣaḥīḥ al-Bukhārī,* #12; *Ṣaḥīḥ Muslim,* #45; Aḥmad bin Ḥanbal, *al-Musnad,* 3:176, 206, 201, 272, 278, 289.
15. The paragraph before this one concerned Imām Aḥmad's time. This paragraph here concerns Ibn Rajab's. This second paragraph is different because it is an extension of Imām Aḥmad's methodology to the following times. And Allah knows best.
16. This is a reference to a fair [*ḥasan*] hadith in *Sunān al-Tirmidhī,* 2018.
17. This is a reference to the verse: "As for that Abode of the Hereafter We assign it unto those who seek not oppression in the earth, nor yet corruption. The sequel is for those who ward off (evil)" (Quran, 28:33).
18. See *Ṣaḥīḥ al-Bukhārī,* #4388-90; *Ṣaḥīḥ Muslim,* #52; Aḥmad bin Ḥanbal, *al-Musnad,* 2:235, 252, 256, 267, 270, 277, 278, 372, 380, 407, 426, 457, 474, 480, 484, 546.
19. See *Ṣaḥīḥ Muslim,* #2722; Aḥmad bin Ḥanbal, *al-Musnad,* 2:167, 451,3:192, 4:371.
20. See Ibn Mājaj, Muḥammad, *Sunan Ibn Mājah,* volume 2, Dār al-Fikr, Beirut, n.d., #3843.
21. See Abū Dāwūd al-Sajistānī, *Sunan Abī Dāwūd,* volume 2, Dār al-Fikr, Beirut, 1990 CE, #5012; al-ʿAsqalānī, Aḥmad ibn ʿAlī ibn Ḥajar, *Fatḥ al-Bārī Sharh Ṣaḥīḥ al-Bukhārī,* volume 13, Dār al-Maʿrifat li-l-Ṭibāʿah, Beirut, 2nd edition, 9:203; and al-ʿAsqalānī, Muḥammad ibn Ismāʿīl al-Bukhārī Aḥmad ibn ʿAlī ibn Ḥajar, *Fatḥ al-Bārī bi Sharḥ Ṣaḥīḥ al-Bukhārī,* volume 14, Maktabat al-Salafiyya, Cairo, 1970 CE, 9:203.

BRIEF BIOGRAPHIES OF PERSONS CITED IN THE TEXT

(Dates are according to the Islamic calendar, unless otherwise indicated.)

ʿAbd al-Mālik ibn ʿAbd al-ʿAzīz, Ibn Jurayj, an affiliate [*mawlā*] of the Umawwīs (d. 150). He was a superior, trustworthy narrator who possessed fiqh. He has narrations in the six canonical collections of hadith.

ʿAbd al-Jabbār ibn Aḥmad al-Ḥamdānī, Abū al-Ḥusayn (d. 415). A judge and master of jurisprudence. He was chief of the Muʿtazilites, who nicknamed him 'judge of judges.' One of his more famous books is *Sharḥ al-Uṣūl al-Khamsa*.

ʿAbd al-Raḥmān ibn Abī Ḥātim, Muḥammad ibn Idrīs, Abū Muhammad al-Taymī al-Handhalī al-Rāzī (240–323 or 327).

ʿAbd al-Raḥmān ibn Mahdī ibn Ḥassan al-Bāsrī, al-Luʾluʾī, Abū Saʿīd (135–198). Among the greatest Hadith Masters. Imām al-Shāfiʿī praised him saying, "I know of no peer for him in the this world [*dunyā*]."

ʿAbd al-Razzāq ibn Hammām, al-Ṣanʿānī, Abū Bakr (126–211). One of the expert Masters of Hadith. He memorized approximately 17,000 hadiths. His most famous work is his *Muṣannaf fī al-Ḥadīth*, published in 11 volumes.

ʿAbdullāh ibn ʿAbbās ibn ʿAbd al-Muṭṭalib, Abū al-ʿAbbās (-3–68). Son of the paternal uncle of the Prophet ﷺ and nephew of one the wives of the Prophet ﷺ. The Prophet ﷺ supplicated that Allah endow him with understanding of the religion, wisdom, and understanding the Quran. He saw Jibreal (peace be upon him) twice. He was 13 years old at the death of the Prophet ﷺ. In spite of his young age, ʿUmar ibn al-Khaṭṭāb (may Allah be pleased with him) sought his counsel. He lost his eyesight at the end of his life and he died in Ṭā'if.

ʿAbdullāh ibn Masʿūd ibn Ghāfil, al-Hudhalī, Abū ʿAbd al-Raḥmān (d. 32). An early convert to Islam and an emigrant to both Abyssinia and Madinah. He is one of the companions in whom the Prophet ﷺ would confide secrets. 'Umar (may Allah be pleased with him) assigned him to overlook courts and the Muslim common fund (*bayt al-māl*) in Kūfa. He was over sixty years old when he died, in Madinah.

ʿAbdullāh ibn al-Mubārak ibn Wāḍiḥ, Abū ʿAbd al-Raḥmān (118–181). Hadith master, mujtahid, merchant, and traveler. He combined hadith, *fiqh*, Arabic, history, bravery, and generosity. He was the first to author a work devoted to *jihād*. He died returning from battling Rome.

Abdullāh ibn Qays ibn Sālim, Abū Mūsā al-Ashʿarī (d. 52). An early convert to Islam who emigrate to Abyssinia. During 'Umar's caliphate he was assigned to command the city of Baṣra.

Abū Dāwūd = Sulayman ibn al-Ashʿath

Abū Ḥanīfa = al-Nuʿmān ibn Thābit

Abū Mūsā al-A'sharī = ʿAbdullāh ibn Qays

ʿAbdullah ibn Thawab al-Khaulānī, Abū Muslim (d. 62). Successor, legist, ascetic. Imām al-Dhahabī praised him saying "the splendor of Greater Syria" (*rayḥānati al-shām*). He embraced Islam while the Prophet ﷺ was alive but did not meet him. He came to Medina during the caliphate of Abū Bakr (may Allah be pleased with him), and then emigrated to Syria.

Abū Muslim al-Khaulānī = ʿAbdullah ibn Thawab

Abu ʿUbayd = al-Qāsim ibn Salām

Aḥmad ibn Ḥanbal = Aḥmad ibn Muḥammad

Aḥmad ibn Muḥammad ibn Ḥanbal al-Shaybānī, Abu ʿAbdullāh (164–241). Founder of the Ḥanbalī school of law, the epitome of hadith masters, and champion of the sunnah. Imām al-Shāfiʿī said, "I have left no one in Baghdad with more understanding and knowledge, and more scrupulous and ascetic than Aḥmad ibn Ḥanbal."

Aḥmad ibn Shuʿayb ibn ʿAlī, al-Nasāʾī, Abū ʿAbd al-Raḥmān (215–303). The great Shāfiʿī and Mālikī hadith master. He authored many works, and his *Sunan* is included as one of the six major compilations of hadith. It has the highest criteria for authenticity among them after the two *Ṣaḥīḥ*s.

ʿAlī ibn Abū al-Ṭālib, Abū al-Ḥasn (d. 40). Fourth of the Rightly Guided Caliphs. He was the first male youth to embrace Islam. He was the nephew of the Prophet ﷺ and his son-in-law. He participated with the Prophet ﷺ in all battles except for Tabūk, when the Prophet ﷺ delegated him to oversee his own family. He received the caliphate in 35 AH after ʿUthmān. He was stabbed during Ramaḍān in the city of Kūfa. He died three days later, at the age of 63. He was Caliph for four years and nine months.

ʿAtāʾ ibn Abū Rabāḥ Aslam (27–115). He was a Meccan Successor and one of the illustrious legists. He died in Mecca at the age of 88.

ʿAbd al-Raḥmān ibn ʿAmr, al-Awzāʿī (88–157). He was born in Baʿlbak, Lebanon, and became the Imām of Greater Syria of his time. When offered a judgeship, he refused. He once said, "If Allah wishes evil for a people, He opens up to them the paths to argument and bars them from deeds." He died in Beirut where four communities attended his funeral: the Muslims carried his bier, followed by the Jews, the Christians, and the Copts. Al-Shāfiʿī said: "I never saw a man whose *fiqh* resembled his hadith [in rigor] more than al-Awzāʿī."

al-Awzā'ī = ʿAbd al-Raḥmān ibn ʿAmr

Al-Bukhārī = Muḥammad ibn Ismā'īl

al-Ḥākim = Muḥammad ibn ʿAbdullāh

Ḥanbal ibn Ishaq ibn Hanbal. He was a son of Imām Ahmad's paternal uncle. He and the two sons of Imām Ahmad heard *al-Musnad* from the Imām. He authored books concerning narrator criticism. He is one of the transmitters of Ḥanbalī *fiqh*.

al-Layth ibn Sa'd ibn ʿAbd al-Raḥmān, Abū al-Ḥārith (94–175). The chief scholar of Egypt in his age. Imām al-Shāfʿī considered him superior to even Imām Mālik.

Mālik ibn Anas (93–179). The great Madinan Imām and founder of the school of jurisprudence that bears his name. When the Caliph Hārūn al-Rashīd (may Allah be pleased with him) ordered him to come to relate hadith to him, his reply was: "Knowledge is something that is sought, not brought." He authored *al-Muwaṭṭā'*. in response to the Caliph Manṣūr's request for a book of Prophetic hadith. Imām al-Shāfiʿī, who studied under him, praised him saying that "Mālik is Allah's proof over His creation."

Muḥammad ibn ʿAbdullāh, al-Ḥākim Abū ʿAbdullāh (321–405). The well-known hadith scholar and legist. His more famous works include *Al-Mustadrik 'alā al-Ṣaḥīḥayn* and *Ma'rifat 'Ulūm al-Ḥadīth*. The latter is one of the first books concerning hadith sciences.

Muḥammad ibn Idrīs ibn al-ʿAbbās, Abū ʿAbdullāh al-Shāfiʿī (150–205). The great legist and founder of the school bearing his name. As a youth he was excellent in marksmanship, language, poetry, and the history of the Arabs. He then took to *fiqh* and hadith, and became qualified to give religious verdicts by the time he was fifteen years old. Imām Aḥmad praised him saying, "The likeness of al-Shāfiʿī to other people is as the likeness of the sun to the earth." His works include *Al-Umm, Al-Musnad, Faḍā'il Quraysh, Ādāb al-Qāḍī,* and others.

Muḥammad ibn ʿIsā ibn Sawra al-Tirmidhī, Abū ʿIsā (d. 279). The great blind hadith master and author of *Al-Jāmiʿ*. The second most brilliant student of al-Bukhārī after Muslim.

Muḥammad ibn Ismāʿīl ibn Ibrāhīm, al-Bukhārī, Abū ʿAbdullāh (194–257). The hadith master of his generation. He authored his *Ṣaḥīḥ* choosing from over 600,000 hadiths which became the soundest book in Islam after the Quran

Muḥammad ibn Yazīd, Abū ʿAbdullāh Ibn Mājah (209–273). A great hadith master, legist, and Quranic exegete. His *Sunan* is among the six major collections of hadith.

Muhannā ibn Yaḥyā ibn Manṣūr. One of the greatest students of Imām Aḥmad, known for his constant questioning. He transmitted ten or more folios of the Imām's opinions.

Muslim ibn al-Hajjāj ibn Muslim al-Qushayrī, al-Naysābūrī, Abū al-Hussein (204–261). The most brilliant student of al-Bukhārī and the author of the *Ṣaḥīḥ*, the third soundest book in Islam after the Quran and al-Bukhārī's *Ṣaḥīḥ*.

Al-Nasā'ī = Aḥmad ibn Shu'ayb

al-Nu ʿ mān ibn Thābit ibn Zūwṭa, al-Taymī, al-Kūfī, Abū Ḥanīfa (80–150). The great legist and founder of the school bearing his name. He was known for his noble character, sound intellect, and beautiful appearance. Imām al-Shāfiʿī praised him saying: "All scholars depend on Abū Hanīfa in *fiqh*."

al-Qāsim ibn Salām, al-Harawī, Abū ʿUbayd (157–224). A great scholar of hadith, belle letters, and *fiqh*. He was appointed a judgeship in Iraq for 18 years. During his travels, he would transmit hadith from his books. His *Al-Gharīb al-Muṣannaf* is among the first known hadith lexicons.

Saʿīd ibn al-Musayyib ibn Ḥazn ibn Abū Wahb, Abū Muḥammad (d. 94). One of the seven great jurists of Medina. He was born two years after the beginning of the caliphate of ʿUmar (may Allah be pleased with him). He combined *fiqh*, hadith, abstinence, and scrupulousness. He was the most knowledgeable Successor concerning the judgments of ʿUmar (may Allah be pleased with him). He died in Medina.

Al-Shāfiʿī = Muḥammad ibn Idrīs

Sufyān ibn Saʿīd ibn Masrūq al-Thaurī, Abū ʿAbdullāh (d. 161). The premier master of hadith, jurisprudence, and piety for his time. He is, with Abū Ḥanīfa, the chief representative of the School of Kūfā. Aḥmad called him the Imām par excellence and ibn al-Mubārak said, "I learned from eleven-hundred shaykh, but none better than Sufyān."

Sulaymān ibn al-Ashʿath ibn Shidīd, al-Azdī, al-Sajistānī, Abū Dāwūd (202–275). An Imām in jurisprudence, hadith, and other sciences. He was a student of Imām Aḥmad ibn Ḥanbal who recorded five folios of Imām Aḥmad's issues. The Imām considered his *Sunan* an excellent collection.

Al-Tirmidhī = Muḥammad ibn ʿIsā

Ubay ibn Kaʿb (d. 19). One of the scribes of the Revelation and one of six Companions to memorize the Quran during the life of the Prophet ﷺ. He was the most skillful at reciting the Quran. He died in Medina.

Usāma ibn Zayd ibn Ḥārith, Abū Muḥammad (-6–54). His father was an early convert and he grew up as a Muslim. The Prophet ﷺ loved him as he loved his own grandsons al-Ḥasan and al-Ḥusayn. He has 128 hadith narratons. Ibn ʿAsākir wrote that the Prophet ﷺ appointed him leader over an army that included Abū Bakr and ʿUmar.

ʿUthmān ibn ʿAffān, Abū ʿAbdullāh (d. 35). Third of the Rightly Guided Caliphs and one of those famed for reciting the entire Quran in a single *rakʿa*. He married two of the daughters of the Messenger of Allah ﷺ: Ruqayya and Umm Kalthūm, and was thus given the nickname "he of the two lights." He gathered together the Quran which he had read in its entirety before the Prophet's death ﷺ. During his tenure as Caliph, Armenia, Caucasia, Khurāsān, Kirmān, Sijistān, Cyprus, and much of North Africa were added to the dominions of Islam.

Uways ibn ʿĀmir, al-Qaranī (d. 37). One of the early devotees and ascetics. He entered Islam while the Prophet ﷺ was alive but did not meet him. He met ʿUmar ibn al-Khaṭṭāb and then went to Kūfa. He most likely died while participating in the Battle of Ṣiffīn with ʿAlī (may Allah be pleased with him).

Waqīʿ ibn al-Jarrāh ibn Mulayḥ, Abū Sufyān (129–197). A Hadith Master and legist. He was the *muhaddith* of Iraq during his day and perpetually fasted. Harūn al-Rashīd offered him a judgeship, which he refused out of scrupulousness. He authored works in Quranic exegesis, beliefs, and abstinance. Imām Aḥmad praised him saying, "I saw no one more with deeper perceptions and greater memorization. Wakīʿ is the Imām of the Muslims."

Yaḥyā ibn Saʿīd ibn Farrūkh al-Qaṭṭān, Abū Saʿīd (120–198). An exemplary Imām and expert hadith master who has narrations in all six of the major collections of hadith.

Zayd ibn Thābit al-Ḍaḥḥāk ibn Zayd ibn Laydhān (d. 45). One of the scribes of the Prophet ﷺ. He was one of the legists of the Companions (may Allah be pleased with them), and the most learned concerning inheritance laws. During the caliphate of Abū Bakr (may Allah be pleased with him) he participated in the compilation and recording of the Quran. Then during the caliphate of ʿUthmān (may Allah be pleased with him) he helped in copying it. He died in Medina at 56 years of age.

BIBLIOGRAPHY

al-ʿAjlūnī, Ismāʿīl ibn Muḥammad (d 1162). *Kashf al-Khafāʾ wa Muzīl al-Ilbās,* volume 2. Dār al-Kutub al-ʿIlmiyyah, 2 edition, 1408 AH.

al-ʿAsqalānī, Aḥmad ibn ʿAlī ibn Ḥajar (d 852). *Fatḥ al-Bārī Sharh Ṣaḥīḥ al-Bukhārī,* volume 13. Dār al-Maʿrifat li-l-Ṭibāʿah, Beirut, 2 edition.

——. *Nuzhat al-Naẓar fī Tauwḍīḥ Nukhbat al-Fikr.* Dār al-Khayr, Damascus, 2 edition, 1414 AH/1993 CE.

al-Bayhaqī, Aḥmad Ibn al-Ḥusayn ibn 'Alī (d 458). *Al-Sunan al-Kubrā,* volume 10. Dār al-Fikr, Beirut, n.d.

al-Bukhārī, Muḥammad ibn Ismāʿīl. *Al-Adab al-Mufrad.* Dār al-Bashāʾir al-Islamiyya, Beirut, 3 edition, 1989.

——. *Ṣaḥīḥ al-Bukhārī.* n/a, hadith number according to *Fatḥ al-Bārī* edition, n/a.

al-Dārimī, ʿAbdullāh ibn Bahrām (d 255). *Sunan al-Dāramī,* volume 3. Maṭbaʿ al-Iʿtidāl, Damascus, n.d.

——. *Al-Musnad al-Jamiʿ.* Dār al-Fikr, Beirut, 1978.

al-Dhahabī, Muḥammad ibn Aḥmad (d 748). *Mīzān al-Iʿtidāl fī Naqd al-Rijāl,* volume 4. Dār al-Maʿrifa, reprint, Beirut, 1382 AH.

——. *Tadhkirat al-Ḥuffāẓ,* volume 4 in 2. Dār al-Maʿrifa, Beirut, n.d.

al-Ghazālī, Abū Ḥamid. *Iḥyā ʿUlūm al-Dīn,* volume 4. Lajna Nashr al-Thaqāfa al-Islāmiyya, Cairo, 1935.

Muslim ibn al-Ḥajjaj. *Ṣaḥīḥ Muslim,* volume 5. Dār al-Fikr, Cairo, reprint of Maṭbaʿa ʿĪsā al-Bābī al-Ḥalabī, 1376 AH/ 1956 CE edition, 1403 AH/1983 CE.

al-Ḥākim, Abū ʿAbdullāh. *Al-Mustradrak ʿala al-Ṣaḥīḥayn,* volume 4+1. Dār al-Maʿrifa, Beirut, Hyderbad (1334 AH/ 1916 CE) reprint (index vol 5) edition, n.d.

al-Haythamī, ʿAlī ibn Abī Bakr (d 807). *Majmaʿ al-Zawā'id.* Dār al-Kitāb al-ʿArabī, Beirut, 1967 edition, 1967.

al-Hindī, Al-Muttaqī (d 975). *Kanz al-ʿUmmāl,* volume 16. Muʻassasat al-Risālah, Beirut, n.d.

Ibn Balbān, ʿAlā' al-Dīn ʿAlī (d 739), Muḥammad ibn Ḥibbān ibn Aḥmad (d 354). *Ṣaḥīḥ ibn Ḥibbān bi Tartīb ibn Balbān,* volume 16. Mu'assasat al-Risālah, 1414 AH/1993 CE.

Ibn Ḥanbal, Aḥmad (d 241). *Al-Musnad al-Jamiʿ,* volume 6. Dār Iḥyā' al-Turāth al-ʿArabī, Beirut, Mu'assasat Qurṭurba reprint edition, n.d.

Ibn Māhaj, Muḥammad. *Sunan Ibn Mājah,* volume 2. Dār al-Fikr, Beirut, n.d.

Ibn Mufliḥ, Muḥammad al-Maqdisī. *Al-Adāb al-Sharʿiyya,* volume 4. Mu'assasat al-Risālah, 3 edition, 1418 AH/1997 CE.

al-Munāwī, Muḥammad ʿAbd al-Rūʿuf (d 1331). *Al-Fayḍ al-Qadīr Sharḥ al-Jāmiʿ al-Ṣaghīr,* volume 6. Dār al-Kutub al-ʿIlmiyyah, 1415 AH.

Nāṣif, Manṣūr ʿAlī. *Ghāyat al-Ma'mul Sharḥ al-Tāj al-Jāmiʿ li-l-Uṣūl fī Aḥadīth al-Rasūl,* volume 5, index in 6. Dār Iḥyā' al-Turāth al-ʻArabī, Beirut, reprint edition, 1413 AH/1993 CE.

al-Nawawī, Yaḥyā ibn Sharaf (d 676). *Irshād Ṭullāb al-Haqā'iq ilā Maʿrifat Sunan Khayr al-Khalā'iq.* Dār al-Bashā'ir al-Islamiyya, Beirut, 2 edition, 1411 AH/1991 CE.

al-Sajistānī, Sulaymān ibn al-Ashʿath (Abū Dāwūd) (d 275 ah). *Sunan Abī Dāwūd,* volume 2. Dār al-Fikr, Beirut, 1410 AH/1990 CE.

al-Ṣanʿānī, ʿAbd al-Razzāq. *Al-Muṣannaf.* al-Maktab al-Islām, 1403 AH/1983 CE.

al-Shaʿrānī, ʿAbd al-Wahhāb (d 973). *Lawāqiʿ al-Anwār al-Qudsiyyah fī Bayān al-ʿUhūd al-Muḥammadiyyah*. Muṣṭafā al-Bābī al-Ḥalabī wa Awlāduh, 1393 AH.
al-Tirmidhī, Abū ʿĪsā. *Sunan al-Tirmidhī,* volume 5. Dār Iḥyāʾ al-Turāth al-ʿArabī, Beirut, reprint of Cairo edition.

ABOUT THE TRANSLATOR

Musa Furber is qualified to issue Islamic legal edicts (*fatwās*). He received his license to deliver edicts from senior scholars at the Egyptian House of Edicts (*Dār al-Iftāʾ al-Miṣriyyah*) including the Grand Mufti of Egypt. He studied traditional Islamic disciplines for over 15 years with numerous scholars in Damascus, Cairo, and elsewhere. He also holds a BA in Applied Linguistics from Portland State University, and an MPA from Dubai School of Government. He currently resides in Abu Dhabi, UAE.

63205014R00029

Made in the USA
Charleston, SC
31 October 2016